WHAT

MAKES

A CHURCH

EVANGELICAL?

TODAY'S
ISSUES

WHAT

MAKES

A CHURCH

EVANGELICAL?

JAMES
MONTGOMERY
BOICE

CROSSWAY BOOKS • WHEATON, ILLINOIS
A DIVISION OF GOOD NEWS PUBLISHERS

What Makes a Church Evangelical?

Copyright © 1999 by the Alliance of Confessing Evangelicals

Published by Crossway Books
a division of Good News Publishers
1300 Crescent Street
Wheaton, Illinois 60187

First printing, 1999

Printed in the United States of America

The Alliance of Confessing Evangelicals exists to call the church, amidst our dying culture, to repent of its worldliness, to recover and confess the truth of God's Word as did the Reformers, and to see that truth embodied in doctrine, worship and life.

Library of Congress Cataloging-in-Publication Data
Boice, James Montgomery, 1938–
   What makes a church evangelical? / James Montgomery Boice.
   p.   cm. — (Today's issues)
   Includes bibliographical references.
   ISBN 1-58134-049-4 (booklet)
   1. Evangelicalism. 2. Theology, Doctrinal.   I. Title.
BR1640.B65   1999
230'.04624—dc21   99-11515
                                                          CIP

13	12	11	10	09	08	07	06	05	04	03	02	01	00	99
15	14	13	12	11	10	9	8	7	6	5	4	3	2	1

CONTENTS

PREFACE

These are not good days for the evangelical church, and anyone who steps back from what is going on for a moment to try to evaluate our life and times will understand that.

In the last few years a number of important books have been published all trying to understand what is happening, and they are saying much the same thing even though the authors come from fairly different backgrounds and are doing different work. One is by David F. Wells, a theology professor at Gordon-Conwell Theological Seminary in Massachusetts. It is called *No Place for Truth*. A second is by Michael Scott Horton, vice president of the Alliance of Confessing Evangelicals. His book is called *Power Religion*. The third is by the well-known pastor of Grace Community Church in California, John F. MacArthur. It is called *Ashamed of the Gospel*. Each of these authors is writing about the evangelical church, not the liberal church, and a person can get an idea of what each is saying from the titles alone.

Yet the subtitles are even more revealing. The subtitle of Wells's book reads *Or Whatever Happened to Evangelical Theology?* The subtitle of Horton's book is *The Selling Out of the Evangelical Church*. The subtitle of John MacArthur's work proclaims, *When the Church Becomes Like the World*.

When you put these together, you realize that these careful observers of the current church scene perceive that today evangelicalism is seriously off base because it has abandoned its evangelical truth-heritage. The thesis of David Wells's book is that the evangelical church is either dead or dying as a significant religious force because it has forgotten what it stands for. Instead of trying to do God's work in God's way, it is trying to build a prosperous earthly kingdom with secular tools. Thus, in spite of our apparent success we have been "living in a fool's paradise," Wells declared in an address to the National Association of Evangelicals in 1995.

John H. Armstrong, a founding member of the Alliance of Confessing Evangelicals, has edited a volume titled *The Coming Evangelical Crisis*. When he was asked not long afterwards whether he thought the crisis was still coming or is actually here, he admitted that in his judgment the crisis is already upon us.

The Alliance of Confessing Evangelicals is addressing this problem through seminars and conferences, radio programs, *modern* REFORMATION magazine, Reformation Societies, and scholarly writings. The series of booklets on today's issues, of which this is the first, is a further effort along these same lines. If you are troubled by the state of today's church and are helped by these booklets, we invite you to contact the Alliance at 1716 Spruce Street, Philadelphia, PA 19103. You can also phone us at 215-546-3696 or visit the Alliance at our website: www.AllianceNet.org. We would like to work with you under God "for a modern Reformation."

James Montgomery Boice
President, Alliance of Confessing Evangelicals
Series Editor

ONE

A Thirty-Year
Perspective

When I returned to the United States from theological studies in Europe in 1966 to work at *Christianity Today*, I found that it was a time of rising influence for evangelicals. *Christianity Today* was part of the resurgence. Under the leadership of its first editor Carl F. H. Henry the magazine was mounting an effective challenge to the liberal churches and especially to the liberal theological thought journal *Christian Century*. Evangelical churches were growing, and they were emerging from their comfortable suburban ghettos to engage selected aspects of the secular culture.

Observing this trend a decade later, *Newsweek* magazine would call 1976 "the year of the evangelical."

The Worldly Liberal Churches

It was also a time of decline for the mainline churches. I was part of one of those denominations from 1968 to 1980, and I came to the conclusion that the mainline churches were trying to do God's work in a secular way and that they were declining as a result. The older churches were pursuing the world's wisdom, embracing the world's theology, following the world's agenda, and employing the world's methods.

1. *The world's wisdom*. In earlier ages of the

church Christians stood before their Bibles and confessed their ignorance of spiritual things. They even confessed their inability to understand what was written in the Bible except for the grace of God through the ministry of the Holy Spirit to unfold the Bible's wisdom to them. They sought the wisdom of God in Scripture. But this ancient wisdom had been set aside by liberal churches with the result that the reforming voice of God in the church through the Scriptures was forgotten.

This had three sad consequences for these churches. First, it produced a state of uncertainty about what to believe by church leaders. This was usually covered up, but it was the true case, and it explained why so many people were beginning to desert these churches and turn to conservative churches instead. People are not attracted to churches that do not know what they believe. Second, the liberal churches were embracing the outlook and moral values of the world. Since there was nothing to make them distinct, they ended up being merely a pale reflection of the culture in which they were functioning. Third, they made decisions based not on the teachings of the Bible but as a response to the prevailing opinions of the time, what I called the wisdom of the 51 percent vote. Business was done by consensus. I learned that if Christians throw out a transcendent authority, another authority will come in to take the Bible's place.

2. *The world's theology.* The mainline churches had also adopted the world's theology. The world's theology is easy to define. It is the view that human beings are basically good, that no one is really lost, and that belief in Jesus Christ is not necessary for anyone's salvation, though it may be helpful for some people.

In this approach many of the old biblical terms were retained, but they were given different meanings. *Sin* became not rebellion against God and his righteous law, for which we are held accountable, but ignorance or the oppression found in social structures. The way to overcome it was by social change, new laws, or revolution. *Jesus* became not the incarnate God who died for our salvation, but rather a pattern for creative living. We were to look to Jesus as an example, but not as a divine Savior. *Salvation* was defined as liberation from oppressive social structures. *Faith* meant becoming aware of oppression and beginning to do something about it. *Evangelism* did not mean carrying the Gospel of Jesus Christ to a perishing world, but rather working through the world's power centers to overthrow injustice.

3. *The world's agenda.* In the liberal churches the words "the world must set the agenda" were quite popular. They meant that the church's concerns should be the concerns of the world, even to the exclusion of the Gospel. If the world's main priority was world hunger, that should be the church's priority too. Racism? Ecology? Aging? Whatever it was, it was to be first in the concerns of Christian people.

4. *The world's methods.* The final capitulation of the mainline churches to the world was in the area of methods. The methods God has given for us to do his work are: (a) participation, (b) persuasion, and (c) prayer. But these three methods, particularly persuasion and prayer, were being jettisoned by the mainline churches as hopelessly inadequate, and what was proposed in their place was a gospel of power politics and money. I saw a cartoon that appeared in *The New Yorker* at about that time that I thought got it exactly right. Two Pilgrims were coming over on the Mayflower, and one was saying to the other, "Religious freedom is my immediate goal, but my long-range plan is to go into real estate."

The Worldly Evangelical Churches

What has hit me like a thunderbolt in recent years is the discovery that what I had been saying about the liberal churches at the end of the 1960s and in the 1970s now needs to be said about the evangelical churches too.

Can it be that evangelicals, who have always opposed liberalism and its methods, have fixed their eyes on a worldly kingdom and have made politics and money their weapons of choice for winning it? I think they have. A few years ago Martin Marty, always a shrewd observer of the American church, said in a magazine interview that in his judgment, by the end of the century evangelicals would be "the most worldly people in America." He was on target when he said that, except that he was probably a bit too nice. Evangelicals have already fulfilled his prophecy, and it is not yet the year 2000.

1. *The world's wisdom.* Evangelicals are not heretics, at least not consciously. If we ask whether the Bible is the authoritative and inerrant Word of God, most will answer affirmatively. But many evangelicals have abandoned the Bible all the same simply because they do not think it is adequate for the challenges we face as we come to the end of the twentieth century. They do not think it is sufficient for winning people to Christ; so they turn to felt-need sermons or entertainment or signs and wonders instead. They do not think it is sufficient for achieving Christian growth; so they turn to therapy groups or Christian counseling.

2. *The world's theology.* Like the liberals before us, evangelicals use the Bible's words but give them new meaning, pouring bad secular content into spiritual terminology. *Sin* becomes dysfunctional behavior. *Salvation* becomes self-esteem or wholeness. *Jesus* becomes more of an example for right living than our Savior from sin. People are told how to have happy marriages and raise nice children, but not how to get right with an offended God.

3. *The world's agenda.* The world's major

agenda—forget world hunger, racism, or ecology—is to be happy, happiness being understood as the maximum amount of personal peace and sufficient prosperity to enjoy it. But is that not the bottom line of much evangelical preaching today? To be happy? To be content? To be satisfied? Far be it from us to preach a gospel that would expose people's sins and drive them to the Savior.

4. *The world's methods*. Evangelicals have become like liberals in this area too. How else are we to explain the stress so many place on numerical growth and money? That so many pastors tone down the hard edges of Bible truth in order to attract greater numbers to their services? That we support a National Association of Evangelicals lobby in Washington? Or that we have created social action groups to advance specific legislation?

Or consider evangelical rhetoric. Evangelicals speak of "taking back America," "fighting for the country's soul," "reclaiming the United States for Christ." How? By electing Christian presidents, congressmen, and senators, lobbying for conservative judges, taking over power structures, and imposing our Christian standard of morality on the rest of the nation by law. Was America ever really a Christian nation? Was any nation? And does law produce morality? What about Augustine's doctrine of the two cities that meant so much to the Reformers? Will any country ever be anything other than man's city? And what about America's soul? Is there really an American soul to be redeemed? Or fought over?

When you put these contemporary evangelical characteristics together it is hard to escape feeling that today's evangelicals sound much like the old *Christian Century* that *Christianity Today* was founded to oppose.

TWO

Reviving Evangelicalism

Part of the problem is the onslaught of the modern age. The dominant philosophy of today's generation is relativism, the rejection of absolutes that Allan Bloom decried in his best-selling book on the decline of American higher education, *The Closing of the American Mind*. And hard on the heels of philosophical relativism came the militant attack on beliefs or values of any kind, known popularly as Postmodernity.

The Spirit of This Age

Evangelicals seem to have succumbed to this spirit. Several decades ago, when the conservative rebirth was getting underway, evangelical churches and organizations were held together by varieties of a typical "creed" or statement of faith. It usually had about twelve points, starting with God or the Bible, affirming the deity of Christ, his virgin birth and resurrection, acknowledging the Great Commission, and concluding with statements about Christ's visible, bodily return and the final judgment. These "creeds" avoided any serious references to the church, ignored the sacraments, and never stressed the sovereignty of God in salvation or the inability of unregenerate people to respond to the Gospel apart from God's grace.

In spite of their glaring weaknesses, especially

when compared to the powerful creeds of the Reformation, these evangelical faith statements worked fairly well at holding evangelicals to a supernatural Gospel and to certain non-negotiable essentials. But evangelical strength actually lay in the fact that the people involved knew more of their Bibles and had deeper theological commitments than their creeds suggested. Most were part of some tradition going back to the Reformation. Many people, even if they were not actually Christians, held to something like a Christian worldview.

Today in a secular and increasingly hostile culture we are finding that mild evangelical consensus statements are inadequate. Christians need a robust, full-orbed theology with a great view of God and an informed focus on the doctrines of God's grace. For all its apparent strength evangelicalism was weak at the center, and the result has been the surrender to the world's wisdom, theology, agenda, and methods that I mentioned earlier.

The Alliance of Confessing Evangelicals

Is the situation hopeless? Some would say so, but nothing can ever be hopeless where God and the Gospel are concerned. Therefore, in 1994 a group of concerned evangelical leaders joined to form the Alliance of Confessing Evangelicals as an attempt to revive declining Evangelicalism. After an informal meeting in Philadelphia in February 1994, a larger group of fifteen leaders met in September of that year for a strategic planning conference in Orlando, Florida, where discussion of common concerns gave birth to the new organization. They adopted the following mission statement:

> The Alliance of Confessing Evangelicals exists to call the church, amidst our dying culture, to repent of its worldliness, to recover and confess the truth of God's Word

as did the Reformers, and to see that truth embodied in doctrine, worship and life.

The next step was to gather 120 evangelical pastors, teachers, and leaders of parachurch organizations in Cambridge, Massachusetts in April 1996 to produce "The Cambridge Declaration." The Cambridge Declaration was the product of four days of meetings in which papers were presented on four subjects: "Our Dying Culture," "The Truths of God's Word," "Repentance, Recovery and Confession," and "The Reformation of the Church in Doctrine, Worship and Life." The declaration, which flowed from the papers, argued that chief among the truths evangelicals need to recover are the great Reformation doctrines summarized by the well-known *solas* (Latin for "only"): *sola Scriptura*, which means "Scripture alone"; *solus Christus*, which means "Christ alone"; *sola gratia*, which means "grace alone"; *sola fide*, which means "faith alone"; and *soli Deo gloria*, which means "glory to God alone."

Some matters are debatable, and not everything that is desirable for the church is essential for its survival. But without these five confessional statements we do not have a true church, or at least not one that will survive for very long.

THREE

Scripture Alone: The Formal Principle

Sola Scriptura means "Scripture alone." When they used these words the Reformers were expressing their concern for the Bible's authority, and what they meant to say is that the Bible alone is our ultimate authority—not the Pope, not the church, not the traditions of the church or church councils, still less personal intimations or subjective feelings, but Scripture only. Other sources of authority may have an important role to play. Some are even established by God, such as the authority of church elders, the authority of the state, or the authority of parents over children. But Scripture alone is truly ultimate. Therefore, if any of these other authorities depart from Bible teaching, they are to be judged by the Bible and rejected, even firmly resisted, rather than it being the other way around.

Sola Scriptura has been called the formal principle of the Reformation, meaning that it stands at the very beginning and thus gives form or direction to all that Christians affirm as Christians. Evangelicals effectively abandon *sola Scriptura* when they reinterpret the Bible to fit modern notions of reality or ignore it on the basis of supposed private divine revelations or leadings.

About ten years into my pastorate in Philadelphia, at the end of 1977 and the beginning of 1978, I became chairman of the International

Council on Biblical Inerrancy. That work continued for ten years, until the fall of 1988, and in my opinion it was an important work. The inerrancy of the Bible is a critical doctrine. We were right to defend it, and we had some important successes in doing so. However, important as that matter was, I do not think the inerrancy of the Bible is the most important Scripture issue facing the evangelical church in the last years of this century.

The issue I would pinpoint today is the *sufficiency* of God's Word, meaning, do we really believe that in this book God has given us what we need to do all necessary spiritual work? Or do we think we have to supplement the Bible with other man-made techniques or devices? Consider the following areas of the church's work:

Evangelism. Do we need sociological techniques to do evangelism? Must we attract people to our churches by showmanship and entertainment?

Sanctification. Do we need psychology and psychiatry for Christian growth? Are support groups essential?

Discerning God's will. Do we need extra-biblical signs or miracles for guidance? Does God speak to us "in our heart," in a way that is just as important and real as the Scriptures?

Impacting society. Is the Bible's teaching adequate for achieving social progress and reform?

Unfortunately, it is possible to believe that the Bible is the inerrant Word of God, the only infallible rule of faith and practice, as many if not all evangelicals claim to do, and yet neglect it and effectually repudiate it because we think that it does not really work today and that other things need to be brought in to accomplish what the Bible cannot do.

Sufficient for Evangelism

The first thing we must say is that the Word of God is sufficient for evangelism. In fact, it is the only thing that really works in evangelism. Everything else—captivating music, moving testimonies, emotional appeals, even coming forward to make a personal commitment to Jesus Christ—all that is at best supplementary. And if it is used or depended upon apart from the faithful preaching and teaching of the Word of God, the "conversions" that result are spurious conversions, which is to say that those who respond do not actually become Christians. They become Christians in name only. The only way the Holy Spirit works to regenerate lost men and women is by the proclamation of the Word of God: "You have been born again, not of perishable seed, but of imperishable, through the living and enduring word of God" (1 Pet. 1:23).

The problem is, there are many people who do not actually believe this and who therefore want to lean on other things. Some evangelists, modern-day successors of Charles Finney, depend on certain crusade techniques. Others look to signs and wonders.

In Luke 16:19-31 Jesus described a rich man, who ate well every day, and a poor beggar named Lazarus. Both died. Lazarus was carried into the presence of Abraham in paradise, and the rich man went to hell. At first the rich man asked Abraham to send Lazarus to provide him with some comfort. But when that was said to be impossible, he asked that Lazarus be sent back to warn his brothers, since they were as wicked as himself. "I beg you, father, send Lazarus to my father's house, for I have five brothers. Let him warn them, so that they will not also come to this place of torment" (vv. 27-28). Abraham answered, "They have Moses and the Prophets; let them listen to them." The rich man persisted, "No, father Abraham, but if someone from the dead goes to them, they will repent."

Abraham's final word and the climactic point of the parable was this: "If they do not listen to

Moses and the Prophets, they will not be convinced even if someone rises from the dead" (v. 31). This is a clear statement that people are not converted by miracles, even by resurrections. The only thing that will ever regenerate anybody is the Holy Spirit operating through the preaching and teaching of the Bible.

Sufficient for Sanctification

Several years ago I completed a series of studies on Romans. It had occupied me for eight years. During that time I had discovered quite a few important things about Romans, but the most striking lesson I learned was the way the apostle Paul approached sanctification. It was striking because it is not at all what we would expect or what many people today desire. When we think of sanctification today most of us think of either one or the other of two things. Either we think of a method ("Here are three steps to sanctification; do this and you will be holy"), or we think of an experience ("You need a second work of grace, a baptism of the Holy Spirit" or some other experience). Paul's approach was to know the Bible and its teaching about what has been done for us by God in our salvation.

Paul makes this clear in the sixth chapter where he says, "In the same way, count yourselves dead to sin but alive to God in Christ Jesus" (v. 11). This is the first time in the letter that Paul tells his readers to do something, and what they are to do is "count" or "reckon upon" the fact that God has done an irreversible work in their lives as a result of which they have died to sin (the verb is in the past tense, an aorist) and have been made alive to God in Christ Jesus. In other words, he is referring them back to the doctrine of the believer's union with Christ that he had developed in detail in chapter 5. Before, we were "in Adam"; now we are "in Christ." Before, we were under "condemnation";

now we are "justified." Before, we were perishing; now we possess "eternal life."

This means that Paul's approach to sanctification is to teach doctrine. That is, to live as Christians we must know what God has done to and for us in making us Christians. We must know what has happened, and the only way we can know what has happened is to know the Bible. Then, because we know it, we are to go on with God, acting on the basis of what has been done.

We can express it this way, we cannot go back to being what we were before. We are new creatures in Christ. And since we are new creatures in Christ, the only thing we can do is get on with living the Christian life. In other words, there is no way for us to go but forward.

We can illustrate this in the form of three questions. First, can an adult become a child again? Clearly, the answer is no. No one can reverse the aging process. Second, a follow-up question: can an adult act childish? We know the answer to that because we see it often. Adults often act like children. But here is the third critical question: what do you say to an adult who is acting childish? Women know the answer to that question because they say it to men all the time. They say, "For heaven's sake, just grow up!" That is exactly what Paul is saying to believers. "You are Christians now (if you really are). You cannot go back to being what you were before. You cannot become 'unsaved.' So for heaven's sake, grow up and start acting like Christians."

This has nothing to do with either a method or an experience. It has everything to do with knowing and living by the sufficient Word of God. Is it not true that one reason we see such immature and even sinful behavior among Christians today is that they have not really been taught what God has done to them and for them when he saved them?

Sufficient for Guidance

Not long ago one of my staff gave me a script to be used for an imagined "evangelical hotline," the kind of recorded message one might hear when he or she calls a participating church for psychiatric help. It went like this:

> If you are *obsessive-compulsive,* please press 1 repeatedly.
>
> If you are *codependent,* please ask someone else to press 2.
>
> If you have *multiple personalities,* please press 3, 4, 5 and 6.
>
> If you are *paranoid,* we know who you are and what you want. Just stay on the line so we can trace the call.
>
> If you are an *evangelical,* listen carefully and a little voice will tell you which number to press.

Is that how we are to find guidance for our lives from God? A little voice? Not at all. That is a kind of mysticism. "I prayed about it, and God told me to do the following." In former days a statement like that would have been followed by a more mature believer asking for chapter and verse, meaning, where do you find that in Scripture? We need to get rid of that way of talking and those false claims entirely.

God has given us all the guidance we need in the Bible. So if there is something we want or think we need that is not in the Bible—what job shall I take? where shall I live? whom shall I marry?—after having prayed for God's providential guidance, we are free to do whatever seems best to us, knowing that God, who cares for us always, will certainly keep us on his path. It does not matter what specific action we take as long as we are obeying God and trying to live a godly life.

That does not mean God does not have a plan for our lives in all these areas. He does. He has a detailed plan for all things, having foreordained "whatsoever comes to pass," as the Westminster Confession of Faith has it. But it does mean that we do not have to know this plan in advance and, indeed, cannot. What we can know and need to know is what God has told us in the Bible.

What has God told us?

In Romans 8 God offers a pattern for what he is doing with us, which includes being delivered from judgment for our sin and from sin's power and being made increasingly like Jesus Christ. The five decisive steps of that plan are: 1) foreknowledge, 2) predestination, 3) effectual calling, 4) justification, and 5) glorification (vv. 29-30).

There are also many specific matters.

The Ten Commandments contain the most important of these. It is God's will that we have no other gods before him, that we do not even worship him by the use of images, that we do not misuse his name, that we remember the Sabbath by keeping it holy, that we honor our parents, that we do not murder or commit adultery or steal or give false testimony or covet (cf. Exod. 20). Jesus amplified upon many of these commandments and added others, above all teaching that we are to "love each other" (John 15:12).

It is God's will that we be holy (1 Thess. 4:3).

It is God's will that we should make a habit of prayer (1 Thess. 5:17).

Romans 12:1-2 says, "Offer your bodies as living sacrifices, holy and pleasing to God. . . . Do not conform any longer to the pattern of this world, but be transformed by the renewing of your mind. Then you will be able to test and approve what God's will is—his good, pleasing and perfect will." If we seek guidance—and we should—it is in texts like these that the guidance will be found.

Sufficient for Social Reformation

The final area in which we need to be reminded that the Word of God is sufficient is social renewal and reform. We live in a declining culture, and we want to see the lordship of Jesus Christ acknowledged, justice done, and virtue increased. We want to see the poor relieved of want and suffering. How is this to happen? Not by more government programs or increased emphasis on social work, but first of all and above all by the teaching and practice of the Word of God.

In August 1535 the Council of Two Hundred, which governed the city of Geneva, Switzerland, voted to reject Catholicism and align the city with the Protestant Reformation. Up to that point the city had been notorious for its riots, gambling, indecent dancing, drunkenness, adultery, and other vices. People would literally run around the streets naked, singing bawdy songs and blaspheming God. The people expected this state of affairs to continue, even after they had become Protestants, and the Council did not know what to do. It passed regulation after regulation designed to restrain the vice and remedy the situation. Nothing worked.

John Calvin came to Geneva in August 1536, a year after the change. He was practically ignored. He was not even paid the first year. Besides, his first attempts to preach proved so unpopular that he was dismissed by the Council in 1538 and went to Strasbourg. Calvin was happy in Strasbourg and had no desire to go back. Yet the situation got so bad in Geneva that in desperation the leaders turned to him again, and Calvin returned on September 13, 1541.

He had no weapon but the Word of God. From the very first his emphasis had been on Bible teaching. So he returned to it now, picking up his exposition at precisely the place he had left off three and a half years earlier. He preached from the Word every day, and under the power of that preaching the city began to change. As the people acquired knowledge of God's Word and were transformed by it, their city became virtually a new Jerusalem from which the Gospel spread to the rest of Europe, Great Britain, and the New World.

There has probably never been a clearer example of extensive moral and social reform than the transformation of Geneva under John Calvin, and it was accomplished almost entirely by the preaching of God's Word. If evangelicals are to see their country and culture revitalized today, we will have to recover the Bible as our sole ultimate authority. Once more we will have to become "a people of the Book."

FOUR

Justification by Faith: The Material Principle

The Reformers called justification by faith the "material principle" of Christian theology, because it involves the very matter, substance, or heart of what any man or woman must understand and believe to be saved.

Justification is the opposite of condemnation. When a plaintiff stands in a wrong relationship to the law, he is pronounced guilty by the judge. The condemnation of the defendant does not make the person guilty; he is already guilty. The person is only declared to be guilty. It is the same but opposite in justification. Justification means that the individual is declared to be just or in a right relationship to the Law. If a person could be declared righteous on the basis of his or her own righteousness, the person would actually be innocent. But in salvation, since we have no righteousness of our own and are not innocent, we are declared righteous because of Jesus Christ, who bore the penalty for our sin on the cross and who gives his own perfect righteousness to us, which we receive by faith.

Most Christians know the words "justification by faith" and understand that "by faith" means "by faith alone" (*sola fide*). Yet we have also heard the doctrine described as "justification by grace alone" (*sola gratia*). Which is right? The answer is that both are right since they are parts of the same reality. In fact, we need to add "Christ alone" (*solus Christus*) too, since it is only because of Christ that God can justify the ungodly.

We may state the full doctrine of justification like this: *Justification is the act of God by which he declares sinners to be righteous because of Christ alone, by grace alone, through faith alone.*

This is what Paul teaches in Romans 3:21-26. Those verses include each of these elements. They refer to a righteousness that is not our own but is instead a righteousness from God revealed from heaven (v. 21). They speak of God's grace ("justified freely by his grace," v. 24). They talk about faith; the word appears eight times in verses 21-31. And all this is said to be possible because of Christ alone. "This righteousness from God comes through faith in Jesus Christ" (v. 22), and we are "justified freely by his grace through the redemption that came by Christ Jesus" (v. 24).

1. *The ground of our justification is the work of Christ* (v. 25). This is why Paul includes "propitiation" and "redemption" in his summary of the Gospel ("redemption" in v. 24 and "propitiation" in v. 25 [KJV]). Does God merely overlook sin? No. God's justice is established and vindicated in the death of Christ, because it is only on that basis that God justifies.

2. *The source of our justification is the grace of God* (v. 24). Since "there is no one righteous, not even one" (Rom. 3:10), it is clear that no one has made or "declared [himself or herself] righteous" (v. 20). How, then, is salvation possible? It is possible only if God does the work for us—which is what *grace* means. We do not deserve God's working. In fact, we do not even seek it. Not only is there "no one righteous" and "no one who understands" (Rom. 3:10-11), but it is also the case that there "is no one who seeks God" (v. 11). If it were not for the

inexplicable grace of God, utterly unsought and utterly unmerited, no one would be justified.

3. *The means of our justification is faith* (vv. 25-26). Faith is the channel by which justification comes to us or becomes ours. Faith is not a good work. It is necessary and essential, but it is not a good work. In fact, it is not a work at all. It is God's gift, as Paul makes clear in Ephesians 2:8-9: "It is by grace you have been saved, through faith—and this not from yourselves, it is the gift of God—not by works, so that no one can boast." But although faith is only the channel by which we are justified, it is also the only channel. This is what is meant by *sola fide* ("faith alone"). If faith is merely receiving what God has done for us, then it is by faith alone that we are justified, all actual acts or works being excluded by definition.

Lest We Forget Christ Alone

In 1897, the year of the great Jubilee celebration in honor of Queen Victoria, England was at the height of her colonial power, and the rulers of the empire gathered in London for those self-congratulating days. The Thames was thronged with tall-masted ships, and the lords and viceroys of the empire were reveling in England's glory. Rudyard Kipling wrote a poem for this occasion:

> *God of our fathers, known of old,*
> *Lord of our far-flung battle line,*
> *Beneath whose awful Hand we hold*
> *Dominion over palm and pine—*
> *Lord God of Hosts, be with us yet,*
> *Lest we forget—lest we forget!*

Kipling's "Recessional 1897" was not appreciated. But he was right, and we must heed that warning ourselves, lest we forget the Gospel of salvation by grace alone that is our heritage.

Justification because of Christ alone (*solus Christus*) means that Jesus has done it all, and now no merit on the part of man, no merit of the saints, no works of ours performed either here or in Purgatory (which does not exist) can add to his completed work. In fact, any attempt to add to Christ's work is a perversion of the Gospel and is indeed no gospel at all. To proclaim Christ alone is to proclaim him as the Christian's one and only sufficient Prophet, Priest, and King. We need no other prophets to reveal God's word or will. We need no other priests to mediate God's salvation and blessing. We need no other kings to control the thinking and lives of believers. Jesus is everything to us and for us in the Gospel. We need to center our faith on him alone.

But we are in danger of forgetting that because of our sad preoccupation with ourselves. The polls tell us that the gospel most evangelicals believe in is God helping us to help ourselves. There is little preaching about sin, hell, judgment, or the wrath of God, and even less about the gospel doctrines that center in the cross. Christ and his cross are no longer the focus of our thinking, and because they are not, evangelicalism has become a movement shaped largely by the surrounding popular culture and by sentiment.

The Cambridge Declaration argued, "As evangelical faith has become secularized, its interests have been blurred with those of the culture. The result is a loss of absolute values, permissive individualism, and a substitution of wholeness for holiness, recovery for repentance, intuition for truth, feeling for belief, chance for providence, and immediate gratification for enduring hope. Christ and his cross have moved from the center of our vision."

Lest We Forget Grace Alone

The problem here is not that evangelicals deny grace. We do not want to be heretics. The problem is that although we affirm grace, we nevertheless reject it by neglect.

When the Reformers spoke about grace alone (*sola gratia*), they were saying that sinners have no claim upon God, that God owes them nothing but punishment for their sins, and that, if he saves them in spite of their sins, which he does in the case of those who are being saved, it is only because it pleases him to do it. Today large numbers of evangelicals undermine and effectively destroy this doctrine by supposing that human beings are basically good, that God owes everyone a chance to be saved, and that, if we are saved, in the final analysis it is because of our own good decision to receive the Jesus who is offered to us.

This is why the doctrine of election is opposed by so many. It doesn't seem fair to them. But as soon as we introduce the doctrine of fairness, we introduce a standard of right by which God has to save all or at least give everyone an equal chance of being saved. And that is not grace! If God were motivated only by what is right, without any consideration of a grace made possible by the work of Christ, all of us would be condemned and would spend eternity in hell. For "there is no one righteous, not even one; there is no one who understands, no one who seeks God" (Rom. 3:10-11).

This is also why so many find grace boring.

How can that be? How can a theme that has thrilled people for centuries be thought boring? If you talk to church people about next year's operating budget, you will find them interested. You can involve them in social programs or building a new addition to the educational wing. You can talk to them about the latest baseball scores or Wall Street or a future presidential election. But try to discuss the grace of God and you will find they are suddenly in a field of discourse beyond their capacities. They will not contradict you. They will listen. But they have nothing to contribute. Often you will be met only with blank stares.

What could have caused such indifference, particularly among churchgoing people? It is because of a failure to understand and actually believe four great truths that grace presupposes.

1. *The sin of man.* Modern people do not believe they are sinners. The thought that they are in rebellion against God's rightful rule never enters their heads. All they want is justice, not grace.

2. *The judgment of God.* Most people have lost appreciation for all cause-and-effect links, especially in moral areas. So the idea of a final judgment of God when sin will be punished seems quite fantastic to them.

3. *The spiritual inability of man.* Our culture has taught us that for man "all things are possible." So the idea that we need the grace of God in order to get right with God just seems, frankly, wrong. People assume that it will always be possible for us to mend our relationships with God.

4. *The sovereign freedom of God.* In this day of multiple human "rights," most people assume that God owes us something—salvation or at least a chance at salvation. But God does not owe us anything. The freedom of God to give or withhold favor is the very essence of what grace is about. Most of today's evangelicals think like the secular world around them.

Lest We Forget Faith Alone

When the Reformers spoke about faith alone (*sola fide*), they were concerned with the purity of the Gospel, wanting to say that the believer is justified by God through faith entirely apart from any works he or she may have done or might do. Evangelicals have fallen at this point by making faith into a work by which we are supposed to bring ourselves into a saving relationship with God or maintain ourselves in that relationship. We have forgotten that it is Christ's righteousness, not the believer's faith, that brings him or her into that right standing before God and keeps the person there. Christ's righteousness is put to our account; it is his, but it is accounted by God as ours.

Clearly we must have faith. We can hardly miss the Bible's demand that we have faith in or believe on Jesus. But what is faith? For many, faith is only a mental assent to certain truths, something we exercise once at the beginning of our Christian lives, after which we can live almost any way we please. It does not matter in terms of our salvation whether or not faith makes a difference in our lives. In contrast to such an eviscerated faith, throughout church history most Bible expositors and theologians have insisted that saving, biblical faith has three elements.

1. *Knowledge.* Of the writers on faith, Calvin is probably strongest on this point, because he found it necessary to oppose an error about faith that had developed in the teaching of the medieval church. In the years before the Reformation the church had neglected to teach the Scriptures to the people. So most people were ignorant of the Gospel, even the clergy. How, then, were such ignorant persons to be saved? The church answered that it was by an "implicit" faith. That is, it was not necessary for the communicant actually to know anything. All he or she had to do was trust the church implicitly. The church and its teachings were right, even if people did not know what those alleged right teachings were, and they would be all right too if they just believed in or trusted the church.

It was like the man who was being interviewed by a group of church officers before being taken into membership. They asked him what he believed about the Gospel, and he replied that he believed what the church believed.

"What does the church believe?" they probed.

"The church believes what I believe," he answered.

The committee was a bit exasperated by this time. But they tried again. "Just what do you and the church believe?"

The man thought this over for a moment and then replied, "We believe the same thing."

This was what Calvin attacked, insisting that the object of faith is Christ:

> We do not obtain salvation either because we are prepared to embrace as true whatever the church has prescribed, or because we turn over to it the task of inquiring and knowing. But we do so when we know that God is our merciful Father, because of reconciliation effected through Christ (2 Cor. 5:18, 19), and that Christ has been given to us as righteousness, sanctification and life. By this knowledge, I say, not by submission of our feeling, do we obtain entry into the Kingdom of Heaven. (*Institutes of the Christian Religion* [Westminster, 1960], pp. 542, 544-545)

2. *Assent.* Important as the biblical content of faith is, which Calvin stressed so strongly, it is nevertheless possible to know this content and yet be lost—if it has not touched the individual to the point of his or her being moved by and agreeing with it. The devil knows the Bible and understands it better than we do, yet he does not believe it in this fuller sense. James says that the devils "believe" in some lesser sense, but only "shudder" (Jas. 2:19).

Having stressed faith's content, Calvin added:

> It now remains to pour into the heart itself what the mind has absorbed. For the Word of God is not received by faith if it flits about in the top of the brain, but when it takes root in the depth of the heart that it may be an invincible defense to withstand and drive off all the stratagems of temptation. (*Institutes of the Christian Religion*, p. 583)

3. *Trust.* The third element of faith is a yielding of oneself to Christ, which goes beyond knowledge, however full or accurate it may be, or even agreeing with or being personally moved by the Gospel. Some have been moved to tears at evangelistic rallies but have not been saved. Saving faith is the point at which we pass over the line from belonging (as we think) to ourselves and become the Lord's disciples. It is what was seen in Thomas's confession when he fell at Jesus' feet in worship, exclaiming, "My Lord and my God!" (John 20:28).

Augustus M. Toplady expressed it like this in "Rock of Ages":

> *Nothing in my hands I bring,*
> *Simply to thy cross I cling;*
> *Naked, come to thee for dress;*
> *Helpless, look to thee for grace;*
> *Foul, I to the fountain fly;*
> *Wash me, Savior, or I die.*
> *Rock of ages, cleft for me,*
> *Let me hide myself in thee.*

When those who have been made alive by God turn from their own attempts at righteousness, which can only condemn them, and instead embrace the Lord Jesus Christ alone, rejoice in the grace of God alone, and approach God by faith alone, God declares their sins to have been atoned for by the death of his beloved Son and justifies them by Christ's own perfect righteousness applied to their account.

FIVE

Glory to God Alone: Toward a New Reformation

Each of these great *solas*—"Scripture alone" (*sola Scriptura*), "Christ alone" (*solus Christus*), "grace alone" (*sola gratia*), and "faith alone" (*sola fide*)—is summed up in the fifth Reformation motto: *soli Deo gloria* ("to God alone be the glory"). This is what the apostle Paul expressed in Romans 11:36: "To him be the glory forever! Amen." These words follow the sentence, "For from him and through him and to him are all things," since it is because all things really are from God, through God, and to God that we say "to God alone be the glory."

Do we think about Scripture (*sola Scriptura*)? It is *from* God; indeed, it is God's very own Word. It has come to us *through* the agency of the Holy Spirit by the process known as inspiration, and it will endure forever *to* God's glory. God's Word will never pass away.

How about Jesus (*solus Christus*)? He is *from* God; indeed, he is the true God himself. He has come to us *through* the Holy Spirit, who caused his conception in the womb of the Virgin Mary, and he lives forever *to* the glory of his heavenly Father only.

How about grace? Grace comes *from* God; it is his by definition. It comes to us *through* the work of Christ on the cross and is *to* God's glory.

Even faith is *from* God, comes to us *through*

God's regenerating work in our lives, and exists *for* God's glory.

There are many reasons for the sad abandonment of the Gospel (proclaimed so clearly and faithfully in the Reformation) by today's evangelicals, among them: obsession with the culture, a consumer mentality, and recasting the Gospel in worldly terms to appeal to unbelievers. But the chief problem is that we have forgotten God and are not really living for his glory. In the church of the Middle Ages God's glory was acknowledged but diminished by giving so much false credit to man or to the church itself. Our problem today is that we hardly think of God at all. And the reason we forget God is that we have forgotten the importance of the major doctrines. We do not necessarily deny them, but they weigh upon us lightly.

Haldane's Revival

In the last century there was a remarkable revival in French-speaking lands that started in Geneva, Switzerland, under the leadership of a Scotsman named Robert Haldane. He was one of two brothers who were members of the Scottish aristocracy. James Haldane (1768-1851) was a captain with the British East India Company. Robert (1764-1842) was the owner of estates in Perthshire, and when he was converted in the decade before 1800, he sold a major part of those lands and applied the proceeds to advancing the cause of Christ in Europe. James became an evangelist and later an influential pastor in Edinburgh, where he served for fifty-two years.

In 1815 Robert Haldane visited Geneva. One day when he was in a park reading his Bible, he got into a discussion with some young men who turned out to be theology students. They had no knowledge of the Gospel. So Haldane invited them to come to his room twice a week to study Romans.

Out of these sessions came Haldane's commentary on Romans, one of the best on that book.

All these students were converted and in time became evangelical leaders in Europe. One was Merle d'Aubigne, best known for his *History of the Reformation in the Sixteenth Century*. We know the first part of it as *The Life and Times of Martin Luther*. Another was Louis Gaussen, author of *Theopneustia*, a book on the inspiration of the Bible. Frederic Monod was the chief architect and founder of the Free Churches in France. Boniface became an important theologian. Cesar Malan was another distinguished leader.

These men were so influential that the work of which they were a part became known as Haldane's Revival. In time the revival spread to Holland where it influenced even the great Abraham Kuyper, who became one of that country's most distinguished prime ministers.

What was it that got through to these young men, lifted them out of the deadly liberalism of their day, and transformed them into the powerful force they became? The answer is, the theme of the very verse we are noting (Rom. 11:36), a proper understanding of God's glory.

We know this because of a letter from Haldane to a professor of divinity at the University of Geneva, whose name was Monsieur Cheneviere, explaining what happened. Cheneviere was an Arminian, as were all the Geneva faculty of that day, but Haldane wrote to him to explain how awareness of the greatness of God alone produced these changes. Haldane wrote:

> There was nothing brought under the consideration of the students of divinity who attended me at Geneva which appeared to contribute so effectually to overthrow their false system of religion, founded on philos-

ophy and vain deceit, as the sublime view of the majesty of God presented in the four concluding verses of this part of the epistle: of him, and through him, and to him, are all things. Here God is described as his own last end in everything that he does. Judging of God as such an one as themselves, they were at first startled at the idea that he must love himself supremely, infinitely more than the whole universe, and consequently must prefer his own glory to everything besides. But when they were reminded that God in reality is infinitely more amiable and more valuable than the whole creation and that consequently, if he views things as they really are, he must regard himself as infinitely worthy of being more valued and loved, they saw that this truth was incontrovertible.

Their attention was at the same time directed to numerous passages of Scripture, which assert that the manifestation of the glory of God is the great end of creation, that he has himself chiefly in view in all his works and dispensations, and that it is a purpose in which he requires that all his intelligent creatures should acquiesce, and seek and promote it as their first and paramount duty. (*Epistle to the Romans* [MacDonald, 1958], p. 552)

Today many are talking about a need for a new Reformation, and they are right to do so. We need it desperately. But Haldane's testimony suggests that the reason we do not see revival today or experience a new Reformation is that the glory of God in salvation has been largely forgotten by the contemporary church, and that we are not likely to see reformation again until the truths that glorify God are rediscovered. How can we expect a revival as long as we are taking God's glory to ourselves? How can we expect God to move among us greatly again until we can once more truthfully say, "To God alone be the glory"?

People Who Cannot Give God Glory

There are many who cannot glorify God in this way, indeed, almost all the people of our day. For example:

1. *Secularists.* The secular people of our day cannot glorify God because they are trying to glorify themselves. They are doing precisely what King Nebuchadnezzar was doing in the days of the prophet Daniel. As Nebuchadnezzar, standing on the roof of his palace, looked out over the glorious city of Babylon with its magnificent hanging gardens, he took credit for all that lay before him: "Is not this the great Babylon I have built as the royal residence, by my mighty power and for the glory of my majesty?" (Dan. 4:30).

Those words are probably the single best expression of what we call secular humanism in all literature. They are a concise expression of that rebellious spirit that sets itself up against God. For when Nebuchadnezzar said, "Is not this the great Babylon I have built as the royal residence, by my mighty power and for the glory of my majesty?" he was claiming that the world he observed was *of* him, *by* him, and *for* his glory, the very opposite of what is expressed in Romans 11:36.

God's judgment on Nebuchadnezzar was terrible and swift. The text in Daniel says, "The words were still on his lips when a voice came from heaven, 'This is what is decreed for you, King Nebuchadnezzar: Your royal authority has been taken from you. You will be driven away from people and will live with the wild animals; you will eat grass like cattle. Seven times will pass by for you until you acknowledge that the Most High is sovereign over the kingdoms of men and gives them to anyone he wishes'" (vv. 31-32). God judged Nebuchadnezzar with insanity, reducing him to bestial behavior.

This aptly describes our world! We think we can do without God. We think we can go our way with barely a mention of him and without any thought of being answerable to him at the last day. But that is insane if God is truly sovereign, and the result is a world of bestiality and violence. We need to see that the world about us, with the glamour we admire so much even as Christians, is an insane, bestial world. Therefore, we need to turn our backs on its values if we are to glorify God alone and take steps toward that new Reformation that is needed in our time.

2. *Arminians.* A second category of people who cannot say "to God alone be glory" are Arminians. Unfortunately, they are the vast majority of those who call themselves evangelicals. Arminians believe in grace. They want to glorify God. They can say, "To be God be glory," But they cannot say "to God *alone* be glory," because they insist on human faith or ability as the final determining factor in salvation.

Arminians know that God will not allow boasting in heaven. But if what ultimately makes the difference between a person who is saved and another who is lost is the human ability to choose God— call it faith or whatever—then boasting is not excluded and *all* the glory cannot honestly be given to God. If in heaven someone should ask an Arminian why he or she is there and another person, who has heard the Gospel and rejected it is not, the Arminian will have to reply, "Well, I hate to express this in heaven, because we are supposed to be spending our time here glorifying and praising God. But since you ask the question, I have to say that the reason I am here and that other person is not here is that I had faith. I chose to believe; he or she did not. I, on my own, received Jesus Christ as my Savior." Thus it is that some of the glory is taken away from God and is given to man.

3. *Calvinists.* Even Reformed Christians need to recapture this true Gospel, since even those who insist most strongly on the doctrines of grace cannot give God all the glory if they are, above all else, struggling to build their own little kingdoms and further their own careers, as many are.

I am a Calvinist. But I testify that in my judgment even most Calvinists are not seeking the glory of God in all things. We say we are. We consider ourselves to be the chief, perhaps even the sole true heirs of the Reformation. But often what we are really interested in is increasing our own small spheres of influence. We too want to be prosperous and happy. Or if we think of Christian work, our true goal is frequently success, defined primarily by loyalty to our own programs, churches, and denominations. We will not see reformation until there is profound repentance for these sins and a radical readjustment of our goals.

SIX

What Can I Do Now?

Can anything be done? The Alliance of Confessing Evangelicals believes that something can and must be done, but it will not be easy. The opening statement of The Cambridge Declaration states: "Evangelical churches today are increasingly dominated by the spirit of this age rather than by the Spirit of Christ. As evangelicals, we call ourselves to repent of this sin and to recover the historic Christian faith."

This calls for three things.

1. *We must recognize and understand the problem.* The problem is that we are "dominated by the spirit of this age." We must understand this at a deep personal level.

2. *We must repent of this sin.* This means that our failure is a sin against God, something for which we need seriously to repent.

3. *We must recover the historic Christian faith.* This will require serious study of the Bible and its theology and may involve a radical reordering of our entire world- and life-view, not to mention the way we have been going about Christian work. At the very least it will mean a new trust in the power of the Holy Spirit to work through the teaching and preaching of God's Word, rather than a frantic search for some tantalizing new methodology to persuade unbelievers to attend and join our churches.

FOR FURTHER
READING

Armstrong, John H., editor. *The Coming Evangelical Crisis: Current Challenges to the Authority of Scripture and the Gospel.* Chicago: Moody Press, 1996.

Bloom, Allan. *The Closing of the American Mind.* New York: Simon & Schuster, 1987.

Boice, James Montgomery. *Standing on the Rock: Biblical Authority in a Secular Age.* Grand Rapids, Mich.: Baker, 1994.

— and Sasse, Benjamin E., editors. *Here We Stand: A Call from Confessing Evangelicals.* Grand Rapids, Mich.: Baker, 1996.

Hodge, Charles. *Justification by Faith Alone.* Ed. John W. Robbins. Hobbs, N.M.: Trinity Foundation, 1995.

Horton, Michael Scott, editor. *Power Religion: The Selling Out of the Evangelical Church?* Chicago: Moody Press, 1992.

Kistler, Don. *Justification by Faith Alone: Affirming the Doctrine by Which the Church and the Individual Stands or Falls.* Morgan, Pa.: Soli Deo Gloria Publications, 1995.

—, editor. *Sola Scriptura: The Protestant Position on the Bible.* Morgan, Pa.: Soli Deo Gloria Publications, 1995.

MacArthur, John F. *Ashamed of the Gospel: When the Church Becomes Like the World.* Wheaton, Ill.: Crossway Books, 1993.

Sproul, R. C. *Faith Alone: The Evangelical Doctrine of Justification.* Grand Rapids, Mich.: Baker, 1995.

—. *Grace Unknown: The Heart of Reformed Theology.* Grand Rapids, Mich.: Baker, 1997.

Veith, Gene Edward, Jr. *Postmodern Times: A Christian Guide to Contemporary Thought and Culture.* Wheaton, Ill.: Crossway Books, 1994.

Wells, David F. *No Place for Truth: Or Whatever Happened to Evangelical Theology?* Grand Rapids, Mich.: Eerdmans, 1993.